There is HOPE

living in an abusive home
making Jesus your strength

by Barbara Bartosh

Illustrated by Jennifer Ledgerwood

Illustrated by Jennifer Ledgerwood
ledgerwooddesign.com

Paperback ISBN: 979-8-9858528-0-6
Ebook ISBN: 979-8-9858528-1-3

www.contagiousovercomers.com
www.contagiousovercomers.com/kids/

Contagious Overcomers
Ministries

TO ALL THE KIDS THAT FEEL ALONE

Jesus is with you during the yelling or the hitting, or the hurting, or the confusion, or the sadness. When it all feels noisy, when it all feels like it's exploding, when it all feels like nothing will change or get better - listen for Him and He will speak to you.

~ Barb ~

PRAISE FOR "THERE IS HOPE"

"I cannot imagine a more powerful helper in the life of an abused child than Barbara's book There is Hope! Her love and compassion for children living in the darkness of abuse emanate from having lived in that darkness herself. She walks them down the scary path of loneliness to safety by walking with them, so they sense her very presence in every step they take in escaping fear. She walks with them through the hurt and shadow of abuse to the healing light and Word of Jesus.

Remarkably, Barbara's approach not only tenderly touches the life of the abused, but it will also make every reader more able to caringly help those who have been abused."

Ronnie W. Rogers, Pastor - Trinity Baptist Church - Norman

"'There is Hope' is an encouraging message of comfort understanding and hope for children. Barbara has done an amazing job of using her heart, History and faith to bring us a book that will highlight this dark subject. There is hope is a must buy for all children; a treasure that will help children know they are never alone."

Kelli Hurst, MA, LPC, Licensed Professional Counselor - Restore Edmond Site Director

WOULD YOU RATHER WATCH OR LISTEN TO
THE BOOK? SCAN THE QR CODE BELOW OR
GO TO OUR WEBSITE. YOU WILL FIND A VIDEO
AND AUDIO LINK OF ME READING IT TO YOU.

WWW.CONTAGIOUSOVERCOMERS.COM/KIDS/

CONTENTS

> WHAT DID I DO WHEN I
> WAS BEING ABUSED?

> WHO CAN YOU TELL?
> (BESIDES 911)?
>
> WHAT DO YOU SHARE
> WHEN YOU DO TELL?
>
> WHAT HAPPENS WHEN YOU DO TELL

> THE ONLY HOPE.
>
> TRUST IN GOD AS YOUR FATHER.
>
> BUT MY LIFE DOESN'T LOOK
> LIKE CHRISTIAN LIVES.

1.

I AM SO GLAD YOU ARE HERE!

This is a hard book. And it's hard for adults, too! Most adults don't like to think there are kids out there who are hurting, and they may not be able to fix it.

Usually, abused children can get help through a system in their city. This system may involve police, doctors, counselors and courts, foster parents—everyone there to protect those who've been abused. But sometimes the system doesn't know.

Maybe you haven't told because you feel nobody is safe. Maybe you haven't told because you're afraid of what will happen afterward. Maybe you haven't told because your abuser has said they will hurt you or your family. Maybe you haven't told because the abuser helps the family, and without them your family would go without. Maybe you haven't told because your abuser says you will be in trouble. Maybe you haven't told because you're afraid you'll get to leave the house but your siblings will stay, and the abuser will then hurt them.

Before we start this book, I want to say YOU SHOULD TELL SOMEONE. Anyone. There are a whole lot of people who can and will help you! But I'm writing this book knowing sometimes that just doesn't happen. Sometimes it doesn't happen right away, and other times it never happens at all.

So, even though I'm now like forty years old, I used to be your age. And like you, when I was your age, I went through a lot of scary, confusing and hurtful things. Sometimes when things are being done to us, we can go get help and it quickly stops. But there are other times that for whatever reason, we can't get help right away. That's why I wrote this book—to talk to the kids who are being abused (we'll talk about that word later) but for a whole lot of reasons, they can't get away from it just yet.

I'll tell you all about myself, what I've learned and why I feel hopeful for you—yes, you—even being in the scary mess you are currently in.

THERE IS HOPE FOR YOU!

Romans 15:13

"May the God of hope fill you with all joy and peace as you trust in him, so that you may overflow with hope by the power of the Holy Spirit."

2.

WHAT IS HOPE?

What exactly is hope? Is it real? Hope is a wish, a desire, an anticipation, an expectation, a want and a confidence that something will come true. Your main hope is probably something like you hope things will get better. You hope someone will stop saying or doing things that hurt you. You hope one day soon your life will look very different than it does right now.

Hope isn't about just making you feel better. Hope reminds you of two things.

The first is, things won't always be this way. It's hard to think like this when you are in the middle of it. But everything changes as days, weeks and years go by. So, eventually something WILL change—you just don't know when.

The second thing is, Jesus. Jesus is not a random idea created to make us feel better. He is very real, and He loves you every second of your life. Everything that hurts now and doesn't make sense in this world can hurt less when we know Jesus loves us. He is our strength when we go to Him. We'll talk about that a bit later.

3.

WHAT IS ABUSE?

So, what is abuse, really?

It's the mistreatment of someone. Abuse is when another person treats somebody cruelly, with violence, fear or inappropriate touching, and usually it happens many times, but sometimes it may only be once. But just because it's only once doesn't mean it's less hurtful and confusing!

If your mom yells your first, middle and last name when she finds out you didn't take out the trash—that isn't abuse. That's a frustrated mom.

If your dad yells a cuss word and gives you a dirty look when he steps on your toy—that isn't abuse. That's a mad dad with a pain in his foot.

If your brother mumbles, "You idiot," because you ate the last Pop-Tart—that's not abuse. He's just mad that he didn't get to it first.

BUT

If you are screamed at and told things about yourself that are NEVER true, like them saying you are, "stupid," "worthless," "dirty," or "good for nothing," (I know there's a lot more AND worse)—and whether you are told those things once or often—that IS a type of abuse.

If someone hits you because they are angry, tired or had a hard day, if you are often hit, kicked, slapped, punched or thrown around—that IS a type of abuse.

If you are touched on your body, even in a gentle way, and it has to do with your private areas—even if the person doing it is your age, a teenager, a young adult, an adult, an old person, a relative, a neighbor or a friend—ANYONE who touches you inappropriately— that IS a serious type of abuse.

John 16:33

I have told you these
things, so that in me
you may have peace. In
this world you will have
trouble. But take heart! I
have overcome the world."

4.

WHY DO PEOPLE HURT OTHERS?

There are many reasons, though none are okay excuses. Hurt people hurt other people. Broken people try to break other people. Sad people try to make others sad. Maybe they were yelled at, beat or touched when they were little, so they continue these actions.

But not you. You can and will be TOTALLY different. You don't have to hurt people. You're going to break free from all these bad things because you will come to understand God loves you. You are going to do amazing things! I believe this with my whole heart.

God made us. And when He made us it was to live with him in goodness, light, and peace. We were going to praise Him, give Him glory, and walk with Him. There was no hurting or wrong or bad at that time, but when sin (darkness, badness) entered the world it flipped everything upside down. So, although our hearts still desire that goodness, we are in a world separated from God and that goodness, so people end up getting hurt.

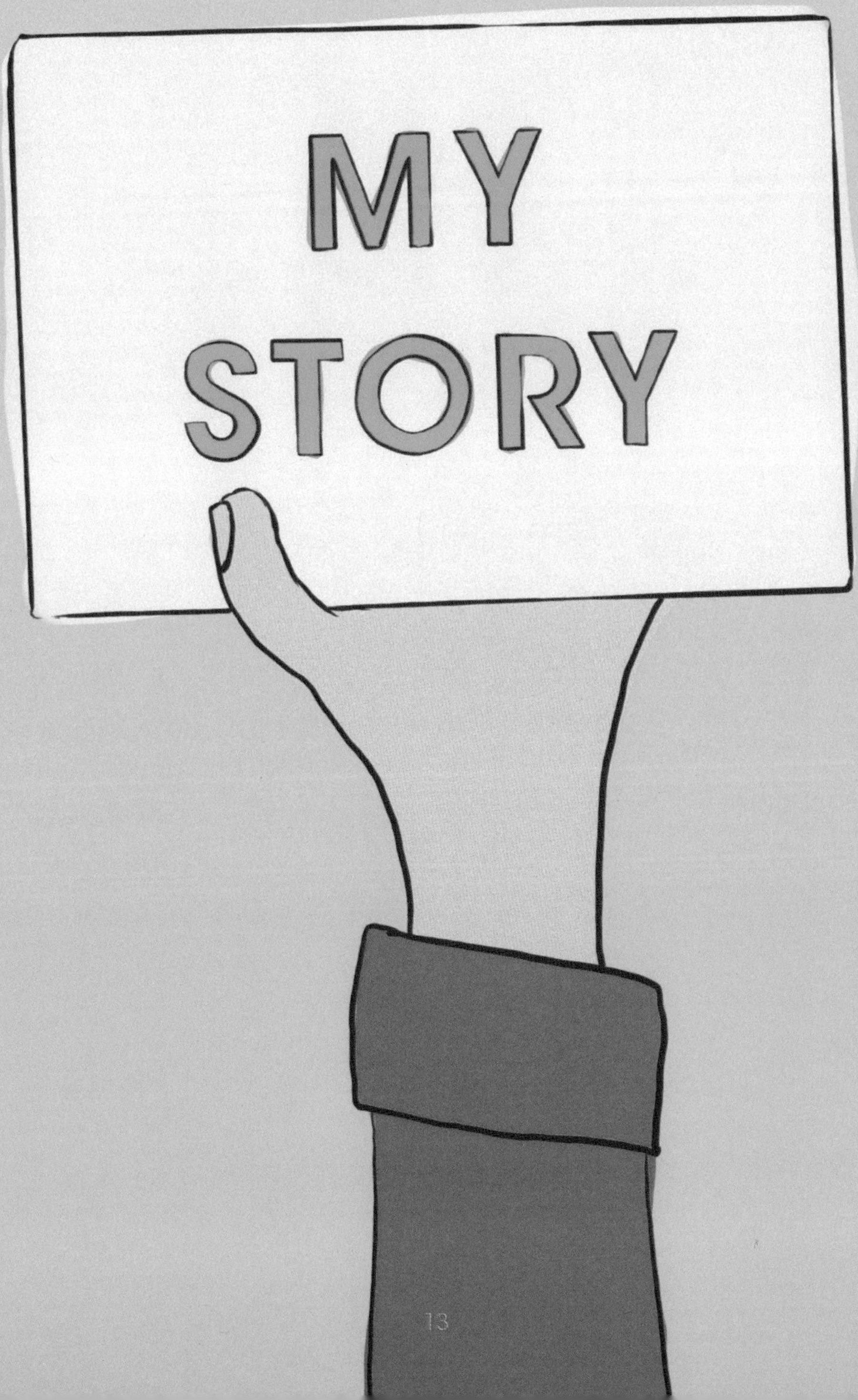
MY
STORY

5.

MY STORY

A few men in my life have hurt me. One hurt me big-time, while the others were smaller offenses. When I was a preteen and a teenager, men took advantage of me. Teachers, adults, librarians, parents, men on the street...

Some would say I was old enough to know better. And maybe I was. But I just wanted someone to love me so badly I didn't care who it was, or if it was safe, or if it was right. I didn't have a relationship with God back then. I understood there probably was a God, but I didn't know what to do with that. I didn't know about the Bible and there were very few people in my life I could go to with my problems.

The main person who hurt me was my mother's boyfriend. He didn't start out hurting me. For the first couple of years, he was really very nice to me. I didn't have a dad who was around much, so he kinda became my dad. I loved him very much, even though he was kind of a rough person.

At my house, there was a lot of talk about sex and people's body parts. We watched lots of movies that showed inappropriate situations. My parents came home with faxes (which are paper memes) with inappropriate jokes. I knew other families probably didn't have all that going on, but that was my life, so what could I do?

One night when I was in third grade, my mother was gone and my mom's boyfriend took a shower with me. That started two years of him touching me several times a week. He kinda treated me like a girlfriend, which made me feel worse because I felt as if I was betraying my mom. I always felt wrong, gross and bad. He never told me he would hurt me or my family if I told anyone, but he did often threaten that we would BOTH be in big trouble if I told. I believed him. I didn't know he would be the ONLY one in trouble and I would be safe.

I finally got tired of it and didn't care if I got in trouble. So I told my mom, who kicked him out. He went to the police himself. After he got out of jail, he stayed away for a while, but then he and my mom got back together. I missed having a dad, and I missed our family having the extra money he provided. I missed my mom being happy, so I said he could move in again if he didn't hurt me. I know that sounds weird, but I think some of you guys probably know what I mean.

He never did hurt me again, but it was really hard and awkward. He still looked at me. He still talked gross. I later learned he talked about gross things with my older sister too. We often watched inappropriate movies that made me feel weird. It was as if there was always this huge elephant in the room that everyone saw but nobody talked about. We just walked around it! And I was always a little afraid the touching would start happening again. Finally, I was able to leave home because I'd graduated high school and went away to college.

Later, I found out he'd been touched by his father when he was a child and he'd never received help for that. Add alcohol and drugs, and he was a very broken person who had hurt me. It's still his fault, but I know he learned it from somewhere.

WHAT DID I DO WHEN I WAS BEING ABUSED?

This is tough. I think it embarrasses some people. I also think it makes people sad. But we have to find ways to get through it right?

These are the things I did or would do now:

- Remind myself that what's being said is not true. I am loved, I am worthy and I am a child of God. These things happening to me are bad and gross, but I AM NOT!

- Remember what's being done to me is THAT person's problem, not mine. I didn't do anything that makes this okay. There is nothing I say, do, wear, walk like or anything else that makes it okay.

- Say rhymes, say Scriptures from the Bible, say riddles, say poems.

- PRAY. Pray it ends, pray for the abuser that they will get help. Pray you will be okay.

- Think of all the things you will do when these things aren't happening to you. Will you go to a friend's house? Go skating? Play a video game? Is there a trip coming up? Will you go to school?

- Dream. Dream up the absolute craziest dreams you can think of. If you could wave a magic wand, what would you be? What would you do? Who would you know? What adventures would you go on?

- And of course, if help is available at that time or there is a chance for you to get away, you should!

Joshua 1:9

"Have I not commanded you? 'Be strong and courageous. Do not be frightened, and do not be dismayed, for the LORD your God is with you wherever you go.'"

THERE IS
HELP

6.

HOW DO YOU GET HELP?

WHO CAN YOU TELL?

It's important to understand that not everybody will know you need help unless you tell them. They may not notice you are acting differently or the person abusing you is treating you in an unusual way. Sometimes we have to tell someone, not wait for them to find out or notice a problem. That may take a long time or never happen at all. It may not be fair, but it is up to us to take a stand for ourselves when others will not or do not know to do so.

- Parent
- Grandparent
- Brother or sister
- Niece or nephew
- Cousin
- Aunt or uncle
- Neighbor

- Teacher
- Police officer
- A friend's parent
- Someone at church
- A parent's friend
- A brother or sister's friend
- Social Media

WHAT DO YOU SHARE
WHEN YOU DO TELL?

The first thing you should do is just get it out. It will be very hard to say those first words, but I promise you, it will immediately make you feel lighter. You can say things such as:

- I'm getting hurt by someone

- Somebody is hurting me

- I need help

- Something is wrong

- Can you help me?

- I am scared

- I am hurt

JUST START TALKING and the adult who is helping you will take it from there. They will almost always help you through it. Just get it out! Then, as they ask you more specific questions, you can tell them as much as you are comfortable saying. If they ask things that make you uncomfortable, you are allowed to say, "I don't feel good about sharing that right now," or "Can we talk about something else? I don't feel ready."

WHAT HAPPENS WHEN
YOU DO TELL?

After you tell the adult you trust, they will ask you more specific questions which you can answer only with what you are comfortable saying. Depending on the adult you tell and who the person is abusing you, the adult may contact another person for help. If the adult hurting you is a parent, they will likely call the police—but YOU ARE NOT IN TROUBLE. They are not going to come to you with their lights on or handcuff you or anything like that. THEY WILL HELP YOU.

If the adult hurting you is not a parent, the person you trust will contact your parents so your parents can help you. No matter what, you will end up talking to the police, BUT the police you'll speak to are experts in this stuff and they know how to make you feel safe while you tell them the hard things. Sometimes they may even bring a social worker with them who will help you. A social worker is someone who works JUST FOR YOU. They are there to make sure you feel safe, and they can even help you tell your story. Remember, you are not in trouble, but they do have to ask questions, or they will not understand exactly what happened to you and now they can help.

What if you tell and that person doesn't believe you? I know there are a few of you who are afraid of that. I hope that does not happen and it is rare that it does, but should it happen to you, you have to go to Plan B. You tell the next person you trust. You tell people until someone listens and gets you the help you deserve and need. It's hard to have to take a stand for yourself and I wish you didn't have to. However, sometimes you do and in this case you make yourself heard!

There are many different things that may happen to the person who hurt you depending on how they hurt you. Sometimes they may just be taken out of your home or away from your life and be told to stay away until things are figured out. Sometimes they will be told to go talk to an expert about what they are doing so they will stop. Sometimes but not always, they go to jail. Remember, it is not your responsibility to protect the person who hurt you. They are responsible for themselves. You don't owe them anything and you do not have to lie for them or help them in any way.

You may not know everything that will be said or will happen after you tell someone you trust, but one thing you can be certain of is that you did the right thing.

LET'S TAKE ACTION

List five people you can tell. Ask one person for help this week.

_____

_____

_____

_____

_____

Luke 8:17

Nothing is hidden or
kept secret forever. It will
be known and brought
into the light.

THERE IS
HOPE

7.

THERE IS HOPE

Like I said earlier, when I was little, I was abused. I didn't know when it was going to stop, or if it would. I was just trying to get through every single day. I also knew a few others who were abused. I had a friend whose dad drank and hit her all the time. One of my abused friends was too scared to tell, and with another, everybody around her knew but looked away. When I told someone I trusted about what was happening to me, thankfully the abuse stopped.

One of the main memories I have during my abuse is feeling as if it was never going to end. The days, weeks, months and years dragged on. Like, was there even another side? I knew someday I'd get older and probably move out, but it might as well have been 500 years before that happened!

And dreaming can be hard. Am I right? It's like, dreaming feels really nice just to keep from thinking about everything happening to you, but can you trust the dreams? Are they even possible?

Do you know that although you are going through bad stuff, God has a plan—a good plan—for everyone?

I totally promise you it's true. I just didn't know it when I was inside all the abuse, confusion, fear, and pain. I didn't know that freedom and happiness were coming, although I wasn't getting it right that minute!

THE ONLY HOPE.

So, who is Jesus? Why should you care about Jesus?

Jesus is the Son of God. I know this story may sound a little crazy. But God created us, and when people started to do things wrong, our mistakes separated us from Him. He is good and He is light, and He can't exist with the bad and dark. So, He sent Jesus to take on all that badness and darkness so we could be with God again. Jesus gave His life by dying in our place for the bad things we have done. The Bible tells us in John 3:16 that, "God so loved the world that He gave His only Son, that whoever believes in Him should not die but live forever." The Bible also teaches us in 1 Corinthians that God made Jesus (who didn't even know sin!) and sent him to be the sin FOR US so we can be made good.

We may not be able to hang out with Him or eat with Him, but He can still be our friend. He can be the One we go to for comfort, for understanding, to talk about fears, and to ask for help.

So why does God allow me to be abused? Is He bad? Did I do something wrong? Does he hate me?

ABSOLUTELY NOT.

Remember, God can't be in the dark and can't be a part of bad. If good and light exist and God is all that, well then, somebody must make the bad and dark, right? That would be the devil. I'm not talking about the cartoon devil or the goofy stuff on T.V. There really is someone who feeds off bad and dark. I don't want to scare you. He is more in the mind. He is in the minds of the people who are hurting you.

I think God allows things to happen because later, there is something we can do with all our hurt and pain. WE CAN HELP OTHERS! I was abused and I would never have chosen to be abused but God has used me to help others and I feel good about that. I can't take away my own hurt, but I can use it to grow and help others grow.

Maybe God has put a calling on your life that you don't even know about yet. Maybe this confusion, pain and fear you feel now is meant to help others. Maybe good really can come from bad. A book in the Bible called Isaiah says that God makes beauty from ashes. I really love that verse because it is so true. I look at my children, my relationship with God, my friends and a lot of other things in my life and I think, "Wow, God! You really did take ashes and make an amazing, beautiful life for me." This could be you too. It just feels very far away right now because you are inside of it all and can't see the other side yet. I get that.

TRUST IN GOD AS YOUR FATHER.

Maybe you have a GREAT father and mother. I sure hope so. Or, maybe you have one great parent and one not-so-great parent. Or, maybe both of your parents have hurt you. The great thing about God is He IS your Father. He is the Father of us all. So, we have an earthly father, and we have THE Heavenly Father. If you lack an earthly father or he is not nice to you, YOU STILL HAVE A FATHER who is in Heaven and He loves you with a perfect love, the kind of love that even if our parents wanted to love us like God, they can't, because they are only human.

Men, especially the men who have acted as my fathers here on earth, have not been good to me. That used to make me sad until I started to experience the love of our Father in Heaven. God's love never confuses me, frightens me or makes me think I am stupid or bad, and I know He is ALWAYS there for me. There is nothing I can do that is so bad He will stop loving me. I am His forever, and you can be His forever too!

When God created people, He created a perfect love in their hearts. They didn't want to or even know how to hurt others. That's the way our parents were meant to be. But sin, that separation from God, came into the world and people started knowing and doing things they weren't created for. Also, we were created with the desire and expectation of receiving perfect love, so it really, really hurts when somebody doesn't love us perfectly. Unfortunately, as long as we're in this world, we will be disappointed by love until Jesus comes again and takes us home. But as God heals our hearts, we can experience great loving relationships with people in this life, even when they are not perfect.

BUT MY LIFE DOESN'T LOOK LIKE CHRISTIAN LIVES.

You may think what you are going through or have been through is super obvious to the world. You may think you're too broken or too dirty to hang out with Christians (people who believe and follow Jesus Christ) or to be like them at all. But Christians are broken, too. Like the rest of the world, some Christians may have more money than you, so maybe their clothes and cars and houses are nicer—but those things don't make them Christians.

What makes them Christians is they came to Jesus broken and dirty inside and put their faith and belief in Jesus and promised to try and follow Him all of their lives. They admitted that they had done bad things (sinned) and confessed those things to Him and asked for His forgiveness. And even after that, they STILL mess up! That's what's so awesome about Jesus. He forgives us and loves us even with all the junk we come with.

Jesus said the church is like a hospital. He didn't want it to be full of super good people, but instead, he wants hurt people to come and be healed!!!!!!!

So, maybe right now you're excited and even a bit scared, but you are thinking, "I want to know Jesus. I believe there is a God and that He sent his only Son to come to earth to take on my sin and brokenness and make me clean again so I can be with God forever. What can I do?"

If you're feeling this way, you can give your life to Jesus Christ! It doesn't take any fancy people or programs to make it happen. You can give your life to Jesus RIGHT NOW. It takes a prayer to surrender or give yourself to God. Surrendering means telling God you may not know what your future holds but you will trust Him to take care of you. In giving your life to Jesus. you are giving all of yourself to Him, and he will bring healing to your hurting heart. Jesus says in Luke 4:18, "The Spirit of the Lord is on me. He has chosen me to tell good news to poor people. He has sent me to tell people who are in prison, 'You can go free!' I must say to people that cannot see, 'See again!' I must cause people that are like slaves to become free."

If you are not sure yet if you believe in Jesus, read the Bible. We know that, "people must hear the message before they can trust God. And people hear that message when someone tells them about Christ." Roman 10:17. Praying a prayer does not save you if you do not believe in Him. But the Bible is ALL about God, and by reading it you will come to trust Him. BUT IF YOU ARE READY...

LET'S TAKE ACTION

Do you believe in God?
Go to chapter 8. Not
sure yet? Find a bible
and read John 3:16.

John 3:16

For God so loved the world that He gave His one and only Son, that whoever believes in him will not die, but have life forever with God.

8.

SALVATION

PRAY TO ACCEPT JESUS INTO YOUR HEART & COMMIT YOURSELF TO HIM.

Dear Lord Jesus, I know I am a sinner*, and I ask for Your forgiveness. I believe You died for my sins** (here you can confess each of your sins that you know about and ask Jesus to forgive you for each one) and rose from the dead. I turn from my sins and invite You to come into my heart and life. I want to trust and follow You as my Lord and Savior

   *(a sinner is someone who has not accepted Jesus Christ & has not been saved from their sins)

   **(a sin is what separates us from God and is the whole reason we need Jesus)

9.

GET TO KNOW GOD.

THINGS TO HELP YOU KNOW GOD BETTER.

- If you don't go to church and your parents will let you, find a church. Some of them have buses that will come pick you up. You can even ask a church member to pray for you!!!!!!

- Maybe a teacher you know believes in God and will talk to you about Him.

- Social Media has all sorts of people talking about the Bible and the hurts we go through. Though, you do need to be careful when viewing these things because not everybody that talks about Jesus is correct. BUT, you can always compare what they are saying with what's in the Bible and pray for God to help you know and understand.

- Read a Bible. Sometimes even if we're in a house that doesn't talk about God, there will be a Bible lying around somewhere. I know it's a lot of words packed tightly and it may feel overwhelming, but if you go to the book of Matthew (about halfway through the Bible) you will find the parts where Jesus is talking and it's super encouraging. Also, a book in the middle of the Bible called Psalms has wonderful poetry in it! If you have a phone, there's a free Bible app called YouVersion.

MEMORY VERSES

Earlier, I listed one of the things you can do while the abuse is happening—reciting Bible verses and poems. Here are some from the Bible. If you memorize them, you will be able to close your eyes and say them over and over during abuse. That is YOU speaking truth over YOUR life! There are even free apps on your phone to help you memorize verses.

John 16:33

I have told you these things, so that in me you may have peace. In this world you will have trouble. But take heart! I have overcome the world."

Isaiah 26:3

"You keep him in perfect peace whose mind is stayed on you, because he trusts in you."

John 14:6

Jesus said to him, "I am the way, and the truth, and the life. Everyone has to know me to know God."

Psalm 68:19

Blessed be the Lord, who daily bears our burdens, The God who is our salvation. God is to us a God of deliverance; and to God the Lord belong the escapes from death.

Luke 8:17

Nothing is hidden or kept secret forever. It will be known and brought into the light.

Psalm 139:14

I praise you because I am fearfully and wonderfully made; your works are wonderful.

John 3:16

For God so loved the world that He gave His one and only Son, that whoever believes in him will not die, but have life forever with God.

Psalm 127:3

Behold, children are a heritage from the Lord, the fruit of the womb a reward.

John 8:12

Jesus said, "I am the light of the world. Whoever follows me will not walk in darkness, but will have the light of life."

Daniel 3:18

God is able, but even if He does not do as we hope and ask, let it be known that we, His children, will continue to love and serve Him.

Psalm 35:3

O Lord, say to my soul, "I am your salvation."

Psalm 73:28

But as for me, the nearness of God is my good; I have made the Lord my refuge, That I may tell of all your works.

Psalm 69:13

But as for me, my prayer is to you, O Lord, at an acceptable time; O God, in the greatness of your loving kindness, answer me with your saving truth.

Lamentations 3:22-23

"Because of the LORD's great love we are not consumed, for his compassions never fail. They are new every morning; great is your faithfulness."

Isaiah 9:1-2

The people living in darkness have seen a great light; on those living in the land of the shadow of death a light has shined.

Psalm 138:7-8

Though I walk in the midst of trouble, You will revive me; You will stretch out Your hand. Against the wrath of my enemies, and Your right hand will save me.

Joshua 1:9

"Have I not commanded you? 'Be strong and courageous. Do not be frightened, and do not be dismayed, for the LORD your God is with you wherever you go.'"

Romans 15:13

"May the God of hope fill you with all joy and peace as you trust in him, so that you may overflow with hope by the power of the Holy Spirit."

DEFINITIONS

Here are some definitions from the memory verses:

Heritage - good things or ideas that are passed down from people to others

Womb - the mom's stomach where a baby is before it is born

Refuge - to find safety in

Bears - to take on

Burdens - troubles or problems

Salvation - to be saved

LET'S TAKE ACTION

Write your new favorite Bible verse below.

_____

_____

_____

_____

_____

WHAT'S NEXT?

10.

WHAT'S NEXT?

What happens after the abuse? After you are out of the house? This is my FAVORITE question! Because this is when we get to dream.

The fact that you were abused has nothing to do with who you can be later! This is SO important! I will say it again in a different way.

IT DOESN'T MATTER WHAT HAPPENED TO YOU! LOVE GOD—HE ALREADY LOVES YOU! DON'T BE AFRAID TO DREAM! YOUR DREAMS CAN COME TRUE, YOU CAN HAVE FRIENDS WHO LOVE GOD, YOU CAN GO TO SCHOOL, YOU CAN WORK, YOU CAN DO ALL THE THINGS THAT WILL MAKE YOU HAPPY. YOU CAN DO THINGS TO SERVE GOD AND YOU CAN DO THINGS TO HELP OTHERS.

Ask God to lead you. He has a great plan for your life and He wants to teach you and guide you.

"Always trust the Lord completely. Do not think that your own wisdom is enough. Remember the Lord in everything that you do. If you do, He will show you the right way to go." Proverbs 3:5-6

"Be happy that the Lord takes care of you. He will give to you what you most want. Let the Lord be your guide into the future. Trust in Him and He will help you." Psalms 37:4-5

All of Psalms 23 is very helpful when wanting God to guide and take care of you!

You may not have a choice right now with what is happening to you. But you DO have a choice of how you act and feel about the abuse after you leave.

You can find a group of Christians who believe in God, who are looking to Jesus to make them whole and feel safe. Other Christians will help guide you, will listen to you and will be there for you as you learn to walk with Jesus.

LET'S TAKE ACTION

Find a Christian in your life or at school? Ask about God this week.

_____

_____

_____

_____

_____

YOU ARE

LOVED
not the abuse

AMAZING
not gross

SMART
not stupid

CLEAN
not filthy

GOOD
not bad

WANTED
not a looser

PRICELESS
not worthless

YOU DO **NOT** DESERVE TO BE HURT

YOU CAN **TELL** SOMEONE

ACCEPT **JESUS CHRIST** AS YOUR SAVIOR

YOU WILL **NOT** GET IN TROUBLE

JESUS IS **HOPE**

THINGS WILL GET **BETTER!**

11.

A NOTE FROM THE AUTHOR

I think that is it. I am very glad you found this book! I think I've told you everything I can think of about all this. The main things I want you to remember from this book are

 HERE.

Take a look at the pages after this. They have websites, phone numbers and even a QR code to scan with your phone that will take you to my social media and website. I have a church locator on the site. There is even a QR code to take you to the audiobook of this and you can hear my voice. You can go to my website and request prayers and tell me about yourself. I have a group of women who have committed to praying specifically for the kids who reach out to me! We want to pray for you!

Bye guys. God bless you ~ Barb

RESSOURSES

12.

HELPFUL RESOURCES FOR YOU!

These are resources for you to use when you are in an emergency or ready to tell. There are people waiting for you to reach out so they can help you.

911

Childhelp National Abuse Hotline
1-800-4achild (1-800-442-4453)
https://www.childhelp.org/child-abuse/

National Center for Missing & Exploited Children
1-800-THE-LOST (1-800-843-5678)
CyberTipline.org

PRAYER WARRIORS!

At www.contagiousovercomers.com/kids/ there is an area for you to ask for prayers! You can give us a little information or a lot of information – whatever makes you comfortable. We want to hear your feelings and thoughts. They are SO important!

We want you to see the people that talk to God about the desires of your heart, your fears, and your pain.

The people in the pictures love you even though they don't know you, and they want you to know how valuable you are to Jesus and to them too!

So, please go the website and talk to us!

BARBARA BARTOSH

LISA BRADLEY

PAULA CARPENTER

AYMEE HATCHETT

CINDY KORDIS

LAURA PERRY

PERRY SMALTS

KATRINA YOUNG

CONTAGIOUS OVERCOMERS KIDS

Contagious Overcomers KIDs seeks to help children in homes where Christ is unknown. To teach them that God is their Creator and loves with perfect love, and it is through Jesus they can have worth, identity, purpose, and fulfillment.

WWW.CONTAGIOUSOVERCOMERS.COM/KIDS/

Visit Contagious Overcomers Kids website where you can: ask for help, ask for prayers from people who want to pray for you, and work on your Bible memory verses with me over video for FREE!

ABOUT THE AUTHOR

Barbara Bartosh lives in Norman, Oklahoma and is the founder of Contagious Overcomers Ministry. Her heart is to serve the Lord and help the vulnerable who will become our leaders, rise to their worth, identity, and purpose in Christ Jesus. She is a mother of three, cat and plant owner, accountant, writer, and really happy.

CONTAGIOUS OVERCOMERS MINISTRIES

We produce literature, bible studies, and even offer speaking engagements to help expose and conquer relational and sexual brokenness through the light of Christ Jesus. We bring freedom to people so they may know the Lord and walk in the identity of His purpose for them. Their contagious overcoming is a testimony to God's love, grace, and might.

MAKE A DONATION TODAY!

www.paypal.com/donate/?hosted_button_
id=9SB9BE4NV3JQA

Contagious Overcomers
Ministries

Made in the USA
Columbia, SC
16 April 2022

58978562R00038